ALFRED THE GREAT AND THE SAXONS

Robin May

Illustrations by Gerry Wood

Wayland

LIFE AND TIMES

Julius Caesar and the Romans
Alfred the Great and the Saxons
Canute and the Vikings
William the Conqueror and the Normans
Elizabeth I and Tudor England
Oliver Cromwell and the Civil War

Further titles are in preparation

First published in 1984 by
Wayland (Publishers) Ltd,
49 Lansdowne Place, Hove,
East Sussex BN3 1HF, England

© Copyright 1984 Wayland (Publishers) Ltd

ISBN 0 85078 422 0

Filmset in Monophoto Plantin by
Latimer Trend & Company Ltd, Plymouth
Printed in Italy by G. Canale & C.S.p.A., Turin
Bound in the U.K. by The Pitman Press, Bath

Contents

1 THE STORY OF ALFRED

A prince in Wessex

Above *Alfred the Great from an illuminated manuscript.*

There was next to no chance of young Alfred succeeding to the throne of Wessex, or so it must have seemed. Wessex was the most powerful English kingdom in the ninth century A.D., and Alfred had four elder brothers. Fortunately for England, in a time of desperate peril it would be Alfred who wore the crown.

The only king to earn the title 'Great', Alfred was born in A.D. 849. It was over 200 years since the

Below *The boy Alfred visits the court of the pope in Rome.*

ancestors of the Saxon peoples, who occupied most of what is now England, had finally driven the Britons into Cornwall, Wales and Strathclyde. Young Alfred was brought up in a court that had links with European kingdoms. His untroubled boyhood included two visits to Rome, where the honorary title of Roman consul was bestowed on him by the pope. Though his health was never good, he became a great warrior, as well as being a devout Christian and a scholar. He was also generous and cheerful.

Most important of all, Alfred was a born leader. This was just as well, for by the 860s it seemed that all Saxon England might fall to invaders from Denmark, Norway and Sweden—the terrible Vikings. The raiders were now putting down roots and much of Saxon England was already under their control.

Meanwhile, Alfred's eldest brothers had died and his brother Ethelred became king. It was a time when the fate of Wessex hung in the balance.

Above *This gold ring is engraved with the name of Aethelwulf, Alfred's father.*

Victory and defeat

Could Wessex survive? East Anglia had fallen to the Danes in 870 and its king had been horribly murdered. Only King Ethelred and his men could save what was left of Saxon England from total foreign domination.

In 871 a great battle was fought at Ashdown on the Berkshire Downs. Ethelred was very religious, too religious some might say, for he was on his knees at Mass when the battle started. When Alfred found that his brother intended to finish the service before confronting the Danes, he left him and led the men of Wessex into action 'like a wild boar'. Ethelred arrived

later and joined in the fray. The invaders were routed and Wessex was saved—for a time.

Later in the year Ethelred died and Alfred became king. Ethelred had children, but the Saxons believed in choosing the right man for the job in a crisis. It was no time for a boy king.

The Danes were soon menacing Wessex again and to gain time Alfred bought them off. They loved money almost as much as fighting. There were five years of uneasy peace, with the Danes ruling much of the country. Then in 876 it seemed that Wessex's nightmare was about to begin again. Alfred bought a few months more peace, and by Christmas 877 it seemed that his kingdom was safe.

It was not. Alfred spent Christmas at Chippenham (in Wiltshire). On Twelfth Night, the heathen Danes crept up on the royal residence and attacked it. Alfred managed to escape with only a handful of followers.

A highly decorated Saxon shield from the Sutton Hoo treasures.

Athelney

Alfred and his remaining followers took refuge in the Isle of Athelney in Somerset, which was then wooded swampland. The famous story of his burning the cakes that a woman had asked him to watch, dates from this dismal time. As he must have had plenty on his mind, the legend might just be true!

If the Danes had captured Alfred and murdered him at this period, Saxon England might have ceased to exist and the English-speaking world of today

Below *Alfred and his small band of followers take refuge in the swamplands of Athelney.*

never have come about. But in 878, the situation changed dramatically. More and more Wessex men flocked to their king, until at last he was able to take the offensive again. A great battle was fought at Ethandune on the Wiltshire Downs near Edington, a fight that lasted all day. The Danes were routed and fled to Chippenham, where they begged for peace, offering hostages to Alfred. The Christian king did not kill his captives—as Vikings so often did—but made them become Christians. Alfred himself stood godfather to the Danish chieftain Guthrum.

Guthrum was very impressed by Alfred and he and his men settled in East Anglia. There were to be other attacks in Alfred's reign, but his kingdom was now secure. In 886, London was seized from the Danes and soon a treaty was drawn up that gave the south and west of England to the hero of Wessex. The rest was called the Danelaw—where Danish law reigned.

Above *Guthrum, the Danish chieftain, makes his peace with Alfred.*

A wise and learned king

Above *One of Alfred's achievements was to start building an English navy.*

It was Alfred's triumphs in peace, as well as his heroic leadership of the West Saxons in war, that made later generations hail him as 'Great'. He was determined to educate his people. Learning had declined disastrously during the long wars. The invaders had destroyed monasteries, which were seats of learning. Alfred chose a number of key books to be translated from Latin into Anglo-Saxon. He saw to it that history was recorded properly in the *Anglo-Saxon Chronicle*, and he himself translated Latin works.

As well as inviting European scholars to England, he brought over fine craftsmen. He collected the best

Left *Alfred saw to it that the history of his turbulent reign was written down in the Anglo-Saxon Chronicle.*

of earlier laws and put them to good use. Meanwhile, he strengthened his kingdom with extra forts and built a navy to combat the Danes. His efforts were not a complete success for there were too few good sailors to handle the big ships.

Alfred never claimed to be more than King of the West Saxons, yet he was recognized as the leading English king. He was a key maker of England and its monarchy. The British Royal Family is partly descended from him; so was William of Normandy, who was to conquer England in 1066.

Alfred died peacefully in 899. His son Edward, and grandson Athelstan, completed his work. When Athelstan died in 939 he could call himself 'King of all England'.

A silver penny from Alfred's reign.

2 WHO WERE THE SAXONS?

Britannia invaded

Their name came from the short sword that they used, the seax or scramasax. They fought with it dagger fashion and they were known as the 'men of the long knives' because of it. They were called the Saxons . . .

They lived along the rain-swept, marshy, desolate shores of the North Sea in what is now north-west

Below *The Saxon invaders sailed to Britain across the North Sea.*

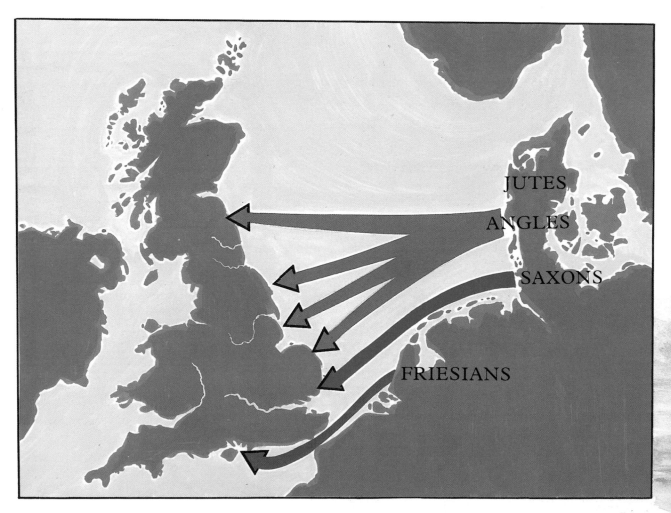

JUTES

ANGLES

SAXONS

FRIESIANS

Germany. Their coastal neighbours to the north and south were Jutes, Angles—whose name was to be given to 'England'—and Friesians. Together they are often called Saxons, for they were the dominant people.

It was a poor living for these tribes, and pressure on them grew from others pressing westwards. Even before the Roman Empire finally crumbled in the fifth century, leaving Roman Britain to its fate, 'Britannia' was being attacked by the Saxons.

The menace was so serious by 340, that a Count of the Saxon Shore was appointed to keep the barbarians out. Britain was also under attack by Picts from the north and Scots from Ireland, while Roman troops were withdrawn to help save Rome. In 410, the Britons were told to fend for themselves.

In their 'foam-cresters' the Saxons rowed to the rich island of Britain. They loved war. That they were also good farmers was not apparent to the beleagured Britons.

Plunder and pillage

The rivers that flow into the North Sea proved ideal for the Saxon invaders of Britain. Returning warriors no doubt told tales about the riches of the island and how good it would be to settle there. Britain's many cities did not interest them: they were countrymen. But settlement was in the future. Now was a time of murder and pillage.

Abandoned by Rome, the Britons—now a mixture of Briton and Roman—put up a heroic struggle and had their triumphs. In 429, a soldier-saint called Germanus, who had come to Britain to deal with some disobedient priests, took command of an army

and ambushed a Saxon force in a valley. The story goes that British priests shouted 'Alleluia!' After this very religious war-cry, the British attacked and routed their foes, many of whom were drowned in a river. Afterwards, the good Bishop Germanus went back across the Channel, having attended to both the spiritual and the military needs of his British flock.

Yet there was no halting the Saxons for good. A writer in Gaul (France) at this time noted that the Britons were falling under the sway of the Saxons. Warfare was not constant. Many isolated areas must have enjoyed years without a sign of the invaders. Yet many Britons probably feared that it was the beginning of the end.

Above *A reconstructed Saxon helmet from Sutton Hoo. Can you see the eyebrows and moustache?*

3 PERMANENT SETTLERS

Hengist and Horsa

In the mid-fifth century, the northern Picts may have seemed even more dangerous to the embattled Britons than did the Saxons. A war-leader named Vortigern—his name may simply have meant overlord—was now king of much of Britain. In this dark hour, he decided to hire Saxons to halt the advance of the Picts.

We have some accounts of what happened next, though it is now impossible to sort out truth from legend. The hired chiefs are said to have been Jutish warriors named Hengist and Horsa. They did their

Below *By the mid-fifth century, Saxon raiders had come to settle permanently.*

job, liked the land they had come to save—they may have been given the Isle of Thanet in Kent as a reward—and sent for their friends!

The Britons fought back and Horsa was killed, but Hengist had arrived to stay, and more and more Saxons poured in. Truth or legend, the basic fact is the same. Now the Saxons had come to settle. From what are now Germany, Denmark and Holland they came from their bleak, overcrowded homelands to a once proud, still rich, but now seemingly defenceless country. With waves of raiders attacking from the north and from across the Irish Sea, what hope was there for the Britons?

There could be none from Rome, herself sacked by barbarians. But there were still some left to fight for 'Britannia'.

King Arthur

Above *A warrior called Arthur was the last great hero of Roman Britain to halt the advance of the Saxons.*

The legend of King Arthur and his Knights of the Round Table was mainly the creation of a twelfth-century monk called Geoffrey of Monmouth. Yet there was a real Arthur, most historians now admit, a shadowy figure who ranks as the last great hero of Roman Britain.

In the late fifth century, the invading Saxons seem first to have been halted by forces under a warrior called Ambrosius Aurelianus. His successor, born around 470, was Arturius, a Roman name that legend would turn into 'King' Arthur. He was never a king, but was clearly a great general.

Piecing together what we can from later documents and from legends, we find Arthur fighting twelve battles in England, Wales and Scotland. He led mail-clad cavalry against Saxon infantry, who wore little armour. He seems to have fought when he could at fords, perfect places to overcome infantry.

Around 500, he won his last and greatest battle at Mount Badon, which may have been in the south-west. It halted the Saxon advance for fifty years. That halt is a historical fact and it is fair to assume that Arthur was responsible. Yet the invaders could not be halted for good. By around 600, the Britons were confined to the south-west, Wales and what is now north-west England.

Above *The pommel of this sword is inlaid with silver and there are beautiful designs of animals, plants and humans. It was found in Abingdon in Berkshire and may have been used in Alfred's battles with the Danes.*

Kingdoms great and small

As more is discovered about Saxon England, the so-called Dark Ages after the fall of Roman Britain seem less mysterious. Yet dark they remain, especially in the centuries before Alfred's reign. Only the patient work of archaeologists is gradually shedding light on them.

Unknown numbers of Britons had escaped westwards, some fled to the Continent. Many of those who were not slaughtered by the Saxons were enslaved; many must have inter-married with the invaders.

Meanwhile, the Saxons built villages and began farming. They were countrymen who liked settling in valleys. The decaying Roman cities did not interest them.

Numerous chiefs ruled, some calling themselves kings. There were many kingdoms, but by the seventh century there were seven—Kent, Essex, Sussex, Wessex, Mercia, East Anglia and Northumbria. You can see them on the map on the opposite page. Some kings claimed to be the 'bretwalda', ruler of all England, but none did rule the whole. Meanwhile, Saxons fought Saxons, sometimes with British allies. Northumbria became the leading power, then Mercia, whose King Offa died in 796 with a European reputation. He built Offa's Dyke, a huge barrier between England and Wales that can still be seen. After him, Wessex became the leading kingdom under Egbert, who ruled from 802 to 839. His grandson was Alfred.

The seven important kingdoms of the Anglo-Saxons.

VIKING RAIDS

1 Dorchester 789
2 Lindisfarne 793
3 Jarrow 794
4 Carhampton 836
5 Hingston Down 838
6 Portland 840
7 Southampton 842
8 Carhampton 843
9 Thanet 851
10 London 851

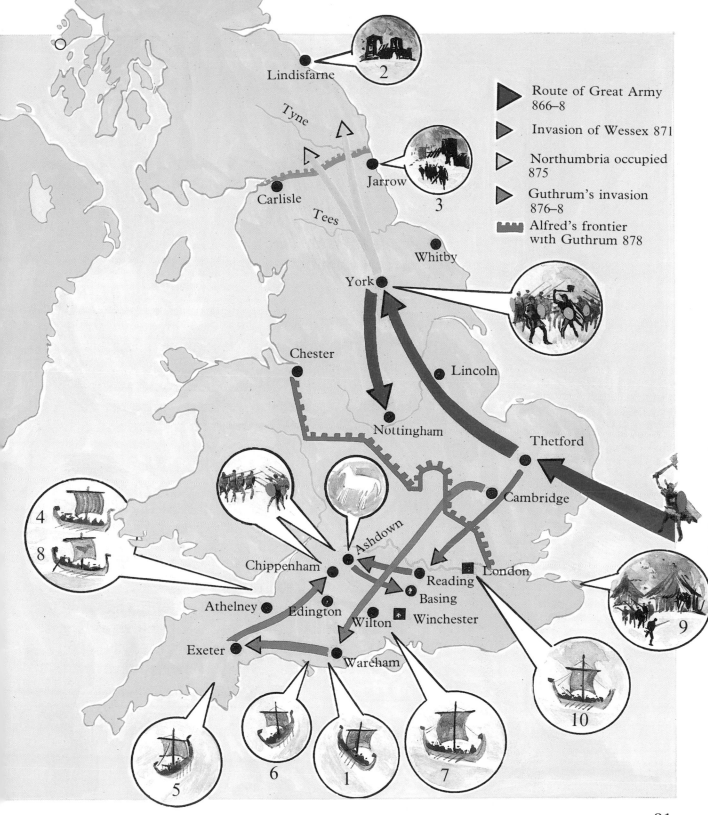

Lindisfarne

Tyne

2

Jarrow

3

Carlisle

Tees

Route of Great Army 866–8

Invasion of Wessex 871

Northumbria occupied 875

Guthrum's invasion 876–8

Alfred's frontier with Guthrum 878

Whitby

York

Chester

Lincoln

Nottingham

Thetford

Cambridge

4

8

Ashdown

London

Chippenham

Reading

Basing

Athelney

Edington

Wilton

Winchester

Exeter

Wareham

5

6

1

7

10

9

4 THE COMING OF CHRISTIANITY

Christian outposts

Life in Saxon England would have been even more harsh than it was if Christianity had not gradually spread across the land. The Roman Empire had officially become Christian in the fourth century, but the Saxon invaders were pagans who believed in Woden, Thor and other harsh northern gods.

Christianity, however, had gained a foothold elsewhere. It had survived among the Britons of the far west; while Ireland was converted in the fifth century by the remarkable St. Patrick, a brave as well as a great man.

Born in Wales or the west of England around 389, he was taken by pirates to Ireland, but later escaped to Britain or Gaul. He returned to Ireland as a bishop about 432 and spent twenty years as a missionary, dying about 460. Naturally, he is the patron saint of Ireland.

From Ireland, Christianity spread to Scotland. A key moment came in 563 when an Irish priest, St. Columba, decided to build a monastery on the island of Iona off the west coast of Scotland. From this spot, missionaries set off to found the Scottish Church. Iona was the centre of the Celtic Church, with no links—except historic ones—to the Church of Rome.

Columba died in 597, the year in which, as we shall see later, the Church of Rome reached the far south of England. Woden's days were numbered.

Left *Celtic crosses were set up in many lonely places in Ireland and Wales.*

Right *St. Columba lands on Iona.*

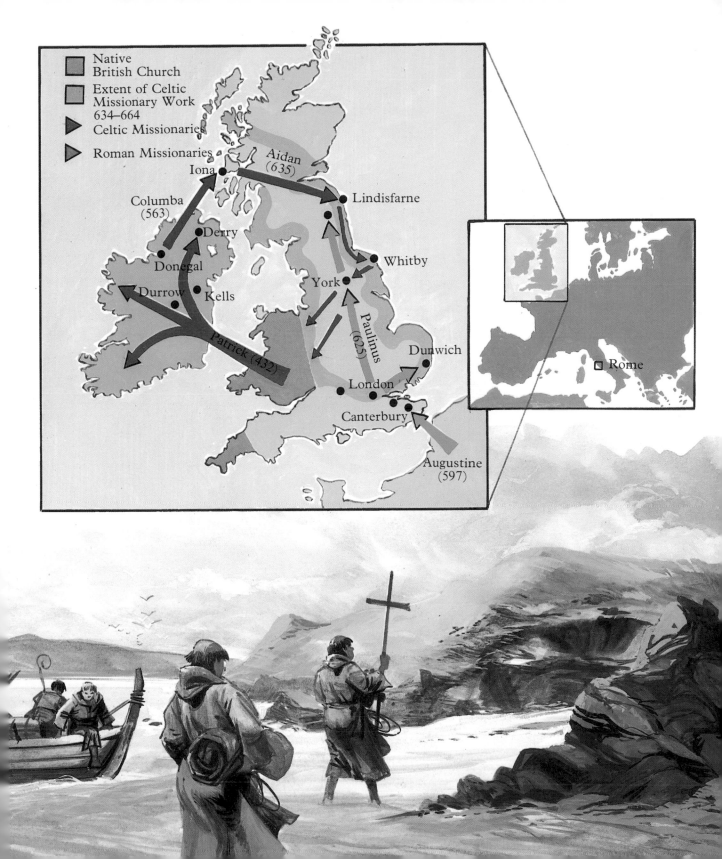

Native
British Church

Extent of Celtic
Missionary Work
634–664

Celtic Missionaries

Roman Missionaries

Iona

Aidan
(635)

Columba
(563)

Lindisfarne

Derry

Whitby

Donegal

York

Durrow

Kells

Dunwich

Patrick (432)

Paulinus
(625)

London

Canterbury

Augustine
(597)

Rome

Above *Building a Saxon church.*

Below *The Saxon church at Bradford-on-Avon, Wiltshire, is one of the earliest known churches in England.*

The Northumbrian monasteries

The kingdom of Northumbria was formed by King Edwin (585–632) by uniting the kingdoms of Deira and Bernicia. Edwin wanted to marry Princess Ethelburga of Kent, whose father Ethelbert had become a Christian (see page 26). Edwin got his bride after he had promised to let priests into his palace, and in 627 he was baptized by Bishop Paulinus in York.

Paulinus was a Roman bishop, but King Edwin was succeeded by King Oswald, who had been converted to Christianity on Iona. Paulinus went back to Kent and from Iona Aidan came to replace him. He founded the great monastery on Lindisfarne, off the Northumbrian coast.

Aidan, a member of the Celtic Church, which was ruled by abbots, not directly from Rome, made the monasteries of Northumbria famous seats of learning. The greatest of all Northumbrian—and Anglo-Saxon—scholars was the Venerable Bede, born about 673. Working in the monastery at Jarrow, he wrote many books and is known as the Father of English History. From our point of view, his greatest work was his *History of the English Church and People*, written in Latin. King Alfred later translated it into Anglo-Saxon. Most of what we know of the early history of England is due to this great man, who died in 735. He had just finished translating St. John's Gospel into Anglo-Saxon.

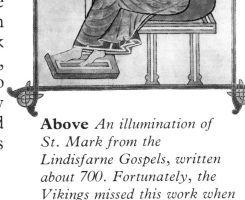

Above *An illumination of St. Mark from the Lindisfarne Gospels, written about 700. Fortunately, the Vikings missed this work when they sacked the monastery in 793.*

Left *The Venerable Bede at work in the monastery at Jarrow.*

St. Augustine

The success of the Celtic Church in northern England was noted by the Church of Rome. It was decided to send the prior of a Benedictine monastery in Rome to bring Christianity to the Saxons in the south. The Benedictine prior was called Augustine and he and forty monks landed in Kent in 597. He was well-received by King Ethelbert of Kent, whose wife Bertha was a Christian already. She was the daughter of a Frankish (French) king.

All went well for Augustine and his monks, and we are told that on one day they baptized 10,000 in the River Swale. Augustine became Bishop of the English, first Archbishop of Canterbury and, finally, a

Below *St. Augustine explains the Gospels to King Ethelbert of Kent.*

saint, but his influence did not extend much beyond Kent, Essex and East Anglia.

As we have seen, the rather different Celtic Church was thriving in the north, and in 664 there was a great meeting at Whitby in Northumbria, known as the Synod of Whitby. In dispute was whether or not the whole church in England should be ruled from Rome and part of the dispute was the date of Easter. St. Colman of Iona was the chief Celtic Church speaker, St. Wilfrid spoke for Rome. Rome won. The Celtic clergy unhappily headed north, while the Irish clergy simply refused to acknowledge the result. Yet the result was a good one, with the Christian religion far more widely spread in England than under the strict rule of abbots.

Above *A Saxon bishop with his gospel book.*

5 KINGS, THANES, CHURLS AND SLAVES

The social order

The piratical Saxon raiders, who slaughtered un-known numbers of Britons and drove thousands more westwards, were not led by kings. Many seem to have been bloodthirsty bands of friends bent on plunder and grabbing better lands, though others were no doubt led by chiefs. Down the years, years when Saxons fought Saxons as well as Britons, some chiefs became kings, even claiming that they were descended from the gods of their old homelands.

Such kings had to protect their people, in return for loyalty in war and work in their fields. None of these early kings lived on a grand scale. A king's 'palace' was little more than a wooden barn protected by earthworks fenced with stakes. The Saxons were fine craftsmen who made wonderful jewellery, but, compared with the Romans, their living standards were barbaric in the early years, even those of a king.

Below a king were his thanes—landowners who were also warriors. Thanes advised their king, as did older wise men. They formed the Witan, which you can read about on page 32.

Below the thanes were freemen called churls, though the word does not mean they were churlish in the modern sense. Even if they were the servants of a thane or of peasant farmers, and though they owed military service to their king in a crisis, they had their rights as freemen. Some Saxons did not . . .

An Anglo-Saxon warrior.

29

Slavery

Above *Slaves did all the hard work on a thane's estate.*

At the bottom of the social scale in Saxon England were the slaves. Their life depended entirely on the whim of their owners, for they had no rights at all. Some slaves were war prisoners, others became slaves because of crimes that they had committed. Some were the children of churls who were so poor that they could not support their families adequately. So a child would be sold into a life of bondage on a thane's estate. Naturally, the worst and dirtiest jobs on the land went to the slaves.

Yet at least the slaves could expect to remain in their homeland. Later, when the Danes swept down

Above *Haymaking in Anglo-Saxon England.*

Below *Slaves were bought and sold at slave auctions.*

on England, unknown numbers of Saxons of all classes were seized by the invaders and sold on the international slave market. For many it was like a sentence of death. However, slavery under the wrong master could be harsh enough in Saxon England, with no protection from the law. And the slave could be sold at any time—or, sometimes freed . . .

No slave could own land, but some churls did. They might own a 'hide' of land, whereas a thane would own at least five hides and often far more. A hide varied in size. It might be anything from 24 to 48 hectares (60 to 120 acres) depending on the area of England. Even a single hide, if a good one, could support a family of churls.

6 LAW AND ORDER

The Witan and local government

A Saxon king would expect to get good advice from his council of noblemen and bishops called a Witan—a word which simply means 'wise men'. Further down the scale, there was a form of village meeting called the 'tun moot', where the churl could make his opinions known.

By the tenth century, in the reign of King Edgar, a system of local government had developed. The shires of England were divided into areas called 'hundreds'. Possibly that first meant a hundred farms or so. By Edgar's time there were shire, hundred and borough courts, each shire having a sheriff who was responsible to the king himself. The sheriff's responsibilities included money matters, such as the collection of taxes. He checked that coins were properly minted and raised troops when needed. He was also on the look-out for shady traders.

Even more powerful were the earldormen, the highest Saxon noblemen under the Crown. Each shire was governed by an earldorman, some later ones governing more than one. The word later became 'earl'—and 'alderman'.

The Witan—Witenagemot in full—was not just concerned with advising the king. It was responsible for electing new ones in certain circumstances. And the noblemen and bishops of the Witan could check the activities of a king who abused his powers. As for the laws of the Saxons, they had some very unusual features . . .

Above *An Anglo-Saxon king and his courtiers.*

Left *A Saxon king meets with his Witan.*

33

The law

If you could not pay your wergild *you might receive a whipping* **(above)**, *or a spell in the stocks* **(opposite)**.

To combat the number of vengeance killings in Saxon England, a system was worked out which, however strange it seems to us, was certainly one way of combating crime.

It was called the *wergild* (from *wer*, man and *gild*, payment). Normally, a murdered man's family felt honour-bound to kill the murderer. Instead, the *wergild* forced the killer to pay for his crime in money.

The amount depended on the dead man's rank. For instance, the going rate in many areas for the death of a thane was 1,200 shillings; for a churl, 200 shillings. Churls were more highly 'rated' in Kent than in

Wessex or Mercia. To give an indication of the value of money then, a cow was worth a shilling in Kent, while in Wessex 500 oxen were worth 1,200 shillings. Naturally, if a nobleman killed a peasant, he had no trouble at all in paying. A poor freeman, unable to pay his *wergild*, would be forced into slavery.

Every part of the body had its *wergild* value—toes, arms, ears etc. Woe betide the non-payer! Slander anyone and, if you could not pay up, your tongue was cut out. Burn a building and you might be burnt. Produce bad coins and your hand would be nailed to the door of your mint!

As for the slave, who naturally could not pay *wergild*, his punishment varied from a spell in the stocks to a whipping or even hanging.

7 EVERYDAY LIFE

The Saxon village

Being such fine farmers, the Saxons must have been delighted to find how fertile England was compared to their old homelands across the North Sea. Using iron axes and oxen-powered ploughs, they not only tilled the coastal soils but also began to cut into the inland forests, with their heavier soils. They worked well together as farmers, just as they had as raiders.

Fine carpenters, they built sturdy, single-roomed huts—places to work, storerooms, and places to sleep. Each family had a hall as a living room. These were not big, barn-like halls such as those in which a king and his thanes feasted, but they were home for all the

family, slaves included.

These small Saxon settlements were true communities, the beginnings of many of today's towns and villages. The Saxons themselves had no use for towns. They were countrymen.

Villagers harvested their crops together, though each family had a strip of land. Their pigs were allowed to roam wild, but their poultry, sheep and cattle were rounded up each evening, for England then had wolves as well as foxes.

When one village was completed, some younger men would soon push forward into the forests like true pioneers and seek a suitable site for a new settlement. Meanwhile, a certain number of men were always liable to be called upon to do military service in the *fryd*, or local militia. There was often plenty of fighting to be done as well as farming.

Above *A ceremonial whetstone found at Sutton Hoo. Whetstones were used for sharpening weapons and agricultural tools.*

Work and play

While most Saxons were busy throughout the year working on the land, improving it, and bringing more and more of it under cultivation, others had jobs in the village itself. The blacksmith was naturally a key member of the community, and women and men made fine pottery. You can read about Saxon handicrafts on page 40.

Villagers were expected to keep nearby bridges in good repair and they had to build forts when wars were raging. Many had to be added to those that already existed to protect ordinary people from the Danes.

Things could get hectic for villagers when a king arrived for a brief stay in the neighbourhood, for it was up to the locals to supply him and his retinue with food and drink. The early Saxon kings were constantly on the move having no real capital, and the strain would have been too great if royalty had stayed too long in one place! Later, especially in Danish-controlled areas—the Danes liked towns—there were more large settlements to cope with unexpected royal visits.

The Saxons worked and drank hard and had healthy appetites. We shall be visiting a royal feast, but ordinary ones were lively enough. Anyone who could play an instrument was welcome and dancing was popular. Minstrels and entertainers, some with performing animals, moved around the land and a popular sport was bear and bull baiting. And, naturally, hunting and horseracing were always popular pastimes with the better off.

This carving, made on whalebone, shows the mythical Wayland Smith at work.

Saxon handicrafts

Sadly few facts about the reign of King Offa of Mercia are known, but one of them throws an amazing light on trade in Saxon times. The great Frankish Emperor Charlemagne wrote to Offa in 796 to complain that his people were objecting to the length of the cloaks being exported across the Channel from England. They were too short!

This means that the English textile industry was already flourishing more than 1,000 years ago in what are becoming less and less rightly called the Dark Ages.

Below *Women were in charge of spinning and weaving.*

The Saxons wove wool and flax, but especially wool. Women were in charge of spinning and weaving and shepherds had to protect their all-important sheep from wolves.

Yet even more remarkable than English exports of cloth is the amazing standard of Saxon jewellery. Anyone who has ever gazed at the Sutton Hoo treasures in the British Museum knows just how fine Saxon workmanship was. They were found aboard what was left of the burial ship of a king, possibly King Raedwald of the East Angles, who claimed to be bretwalda of England. He died in 624.

Marvels include a helmet, a wonderful shield, a sword and sheath, battle-axe and some beautiful jewellery and though the ship had disintegrated, marks indicated its outlines. It was a fabulous find.

Yet ordinary Saxons, not just the rich, wore jewellery. Gold and semi-precious garnets were the most used, and coloured glass provided additional decoration.

Three exquisite examples of Saxon jewellery. **Above** *and* **left** *are a gold buckle and a purse lid from the Sutton Hoo treasures.* **Below** *is a brooch depicting the five senses— sight, smell, hearing, touch and taste.*

Feasting

The hall of a king or a chieftain was never more lively than when a feast was in progress. The setting would strike us as simple enough—a gabled, barn-like building, its wooden walls being without plaster, but decorated perhaps with war shields and stag horns. Smoke from the fire in the middle of the hall would go out through a hole in the roof.

The scene must always have been a lively one, whether it was a king entertaining his bodyguard and friends or a lord feasting with his companions. Quantities of meat were consumed and drinking was on a heroic scale! Ale brewed from barley was enjoyed, but mead, made from fermented honey, was liked even more. Honey was the only sweetening that the Saxons had, and so popular was mead that the halls were sometimes called meadhalls.

There was a harp for anyone to play. Poets would recite thrilling poems to the gathering, but even more popular were the minstrels, who would stir everyone with songs of battles, recent and long ago. Enflamed by drink, the guests would roar their appreciation and remember their own and their forefathers' deeds.

Not every feast was a success. The Venerable Bede described one banquet that ended in pandemonium when sparks from the central fire caught the top of the hall. Being made of wattle and thatch, it quickly burst into flames, as the unfortunate guests fled, presumably sobering up as they ran.

Above *An Anglo-Saxon lyre reconstructed from the remains of one found at Sutton Hoo.*

Below *An Anglo-Saxon drinking horn.*

The story of Beowulf

1   Some 1,300 years ago, an unknown Saxon poet wrote a great poem, based on old Norse legends, called *Beowulf*. It starts at the Court of King Hrothgar of Denmark. For twelve years a man-eating monster named Grendel had eaten one or more of Hrothgar's men each night.

2   To help Hrothgar, a Swedish prince named Beowulf and fourteen picked warriors came to Denmark. Hrothgar, though grateful, did not believe they would succeed. Night fell and after some merrymaking and feasting, fear closed in on King Hrothgar's Court.

6   Beowulf returned to Hrothgar's Court in triumph and there was great rejoicing. Then he and his men went home. Later the King of the Geatas of Sweden died and Beowulf succeeded him. But after fifty happy years, a terrible dragon appeared, destroying men, beasts and buildings.

5   Beowulf had been lent a magic sword called Hrunting. A ferocious fight ensued in the muddy depths of the lake. His sword glanced off her neck and the she-monster advanced on the hero to finish him off. She failed, and Beowulf cut off her evil head.

3   Beowulf waited, then, suddenly, Grendel erupted into the hall. He seized one of the warriors from a couch and ate him. Beowulf sprang into action and tore off one of Grendel's arms. The screaming monster, dripping blood, fled to die bleeding in a marsh.

4   Grendel's mother, an even worse monster than her son, appeared at the hall the next night, bent on revenge. Hrothgar's chief minister was seized and taken down into the depths of a lake to her lair. The heroic Beowulf went after her.

7   Once more it was time for Beowulf to act. With eleven trusty comrades he set out to find the monster. But when it appeared from its lair, only one of Beowulf's friends stayed with him. The rest fled in terror at the sight of the fire-breathing horror.

8   The heroic pair fought the giant beast, whose fangs sank into Beowulf's neck. The heroes killed the dragon, but at tragic cost, for the creature's fangs were poisoned and Beowulf's wounds were fatally infected. He died, mourned by all his people.

8 THE COMING OF THE DANES

The fury of the Norsemen

From the eighth to the eleventh centuries, Viking raiders sailed from Scandinavia seeking plunder and excitement. Their homelands were overcrowded and good land was scarce, so they set out in their 'longships', which were so well designed that they could even brave Atlantic storms and waves. 'Viking' possibly comes from 'vik'—meaning 'creek'—for it was from creeks that they started out on their blood-drenched expeditions.

Vikings from Sweden reached and settled in Russia. The British Isles suffered most from Danes and Norwegians. There is an old cross with a chilling

Above *A fierce animal headpost from a Viking wagon.*

prayer on it—'From the fury of the Norsemen, good Lord deliver us.'

We have met these invaders in the story of Alfred the Great. The very first Viking raid was a minor one on the Wessex coast, possibly in 789. The real nightmare began four years later when Norwegian Vikings assaulted and plundered the great monastery on Lindisfarne. Priceless treasures were looted, and monks were either killed or taken away to be sold into slavery. There is a map showing all the principal Viking raids and battles on page 21.

The Saxons, of course, had attacked England in much the same way, but that was no consolation to their descendants. Alfred, as we have seen, saved England, even though much of the north and east remained in Danish hands. Yet Alfred's grandson Athelstan was overlord of Danish as well as Saxon England. By that time the Danes had turned out, as we shall see, to be admirable citizens in many ways—after the butchery was over.

Viking settlements

Perhaps the fact that Saxons and Vikings came from the same northern stock helped the Vikings settle down peacefully and swiftly after the terrible years of slaughter. Like the Saxons, they were fine farmers, and they were even keener traders. And, unlike the Saxons, they were towns people. They made London into a major port, which it had not been since Roman times, and their towns included Lincoln, Nottingham, Derby and, especially, York.

The city was the chief link between the Vikings' old homeland and Saxon England. Wool, textiles and other goods were shipped from York while imports included furs, skins, pottery and wine. The Vikings had cargo ships as well as warships. There were factories and shops in York. There was nothing like it in Wessex.

The Norse 'fury' was still always likely to erupt, as fresh waves of pirates set out from Scandinavia, but Alfred's successors were usually worthy of him—in the tenth century at least. His grandson Athelstan was confronted in 937 with the Scots under King Constantine, Olaf, the Viking King of Dublin, and an army of Norwegian Vikings. Leading men of Wessex and Mercia, Athelstan utterly defeated the triple alliance at the battle of Brunanburh, which was probably in southern Yorkshire. King Edgar's reign (959–75) saw Anglo-Danish England prosperous and peaceful, but, alas, evil times were soon to return.

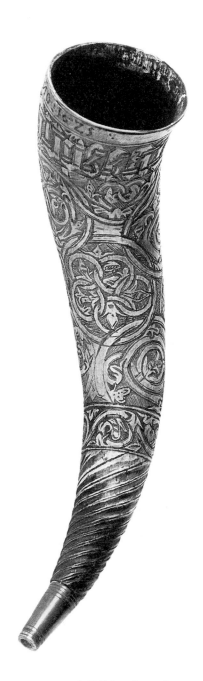

A decorated Viking hunting horn.

Left *Unlike the Saxons, the Vikings were townspeople.*

49

9 ENGLAND UNITED

Few lines of kings have equalled the rulers of Wessex from Egbert to Edgar. The latter's reign is best remembered for the occasion when a crew of subject kings rowed him across the River Dee as a mark of homage. More important was the fleet he built that was noted by would-be Viking invaders. In 975, he died and his 15-year-old son Edward was chosen to succeed him.

Edward was soon murdered, probably by order of his step-mother, whose son Ethelred, aged 10, got the crown. Then in 980, the Vikings struck once more. Cursed with unworthy favourites, Ethelred bought the invaders off time and again with *danegeld*, a tax his

Below *King Ethelred offered the Vikings gold to make them go away.*

Left *King Canute shows up the flattery of his courtiers by sitting in the waves.*

people paid. But he did not, as Alfred had done, then fight the Danes. Known now as 'Unready', he was actually '*redeless*', meaning unwise. He was also not a soldier and untrustworthy.

In 1002, he ordered a massacre of every Dane in England. Unknown numbers of peaceful 'English' Danes perished, one of them being King Sweyn of Denmark's sister. He avenged her ferociously, devastating the Saxon part of England until he, too, was bought off.

When Sweyn died in 1014, Ethelred was recalled from Normandy where he had fled. He died in 1016 and his valiant son Edmund Ironside fought Sweyn's son Canute for the throne. Edmund died in 1016 and Canute became King of England and Denmark—and a great one. The story of his trying to turn back the waves is often misunderstood. His grovelling courtiers tried to flatter him by telling him that such a great king would even have power over the waves. Canute showed what a silly idea this was by sitting on the shore until the waves were lapping around him.

The great seal of Edward the Confessor.

A silver penny showing the head of William the Conqueror.

Right *Duke William of Normandy claimed that Edward the Confessor offered him the English throne while he was on a visit to England.*

10 THE NORMAN CONQUEST

The disputed succession

The great Canute died in 1035. After a wretched period of intrigue and murder, involving the sons of Canute and the sons of Ethelred, in 1042, the Witan chose Ethelred's son Edward as king.

Edward would rather have been a monk and was known as 'the Confessor', so saintly was he. Having been brought up in Normandy, he proceeded to make himself disliked by giving Normans key English posts.

The most powerful family in England was headed by Earl Godwin, who made the king marry his daughter. The Normans in England naturally resented Godwin's power and forced him into exile in

1051. It is possible that soon afterwards, Duke William of Normandy—later 'the Conqueror'—paid a visit to King Edward and was promised the English throne. William's great-aunt Emma of Normandy had been Ethelred the Unready's wife.

Earl Godwin returned later in 1051 and the Confessor handed over the reins of power to him and his family. Godwin died in 1053, which made his son Harold the virtual ruler of England. His brother Tostig became Earl of Northumbria; another brother became Earl of Mercia. Saxon England seemed secure.

Edward died in January 1066 and the Witan elected Harold king—short of royal blood but the right man for the job. Unfortunately, Harald Hardrada of Norway and Duke William of Normandy also wanted the job.

Below left *William also claimed that Harold Godwin had solemnly sworn that he should become King of England.*

Above *The Saxon earldoms during the reign of Edward the Confessor.*

NORTHUMBRIA
(Siward)

MERCIA
(Leofric)

EAST ANGLIA
(Gyrth)

(Leofwine)

WESSEX
(Harold Godwin)

1066

In 1064, Harold had been shipwrecked and taken prisoner in France. He was rescued by his distant cousin Duke William of Normandy and became his firm friend. Later, William claimed that Harold had solemnly sworn that William should become King of England. Perhaps Harold had, perhaps not . . .

As William prepared to back his claim by force in 1066, so did Harald Hardrada. With him was Harold's brother Tostig, who had been chased out of Northumbria for his evil ways. The pair landed in England, encamping at Stamford Bridge near York.

Harold raced north with his 'house-carls', a valiant and loyal bodyguard of Viking descent. Other troops were raised and on 28 September, the invaders were totally defeated at Stamford Bridge, Harald and Tostig being among the slain.

Meanwhile, on the 27 September, William landed and encamped near Hastings with some 7,000 men— Normans from France, Spain and Italy, mercenaries from Flanders and elsewhere. Harold heard the news on 1 October. With his battle-weary men, he headed south, pausing only to raise more troops, and reached the enemy on the 13th. He may have had slightly fewer men, and had no cavalry.

The next day saw the death of Harold and the end of Saxon England. Yet the Normans' descendants became Englishmen, while England had been made by Saxons, Angles and Jutes, so it is wrong to date English history from 1066.

The Battle of Hastings was fought on and around Senlac Hill, some 6 miles (10 km) north-west of the town of Hastings. The English army defended the ridge of the hill, and William's first attacks were beaten back. His army was saved by his coolness and personal bravery. Norman discipline, Norman cavalry and Norman archery played key roles in the outcome of the battle; as did William's pretended retreats, which the English pursued with fatal results—as they were then surrounded and cut down by the Norman knights. Harold was killed, perhaps by an arrow through his eye. His valiant house-carls fought to the death, but by evening, the Normans had won a crushing victory.

SENLAC HILL

SAXONS

archers
infantry
cavalry

NORMANS

The only monument to the last Anglo-Saxon king is this stone which marks the legendary spot where Harold fell.

Table of dates

410 Britons told by Rome to defend themselves.

c **449** Hengist and Horsa land in Kent.

c **500** Arthur's victory at Mount Badon.

563 Columba founds monastery on Iona.

597 St. Augustine arrives in Kent.

617 Start of Northumbrian supremacy under Edwin.

635 St. Aidan founds Lindisfarne.

664 Synod of Whitby.

c **673** Birth of the Venerable Bede.

735 Death of Bede.

757–96 Reign of King Offa of Mercia, which becomes leading English kingdom.

c **789** First Viking raid on England on Wessex coast.

802–39 Egbert King of Wessex.

825 Egbert defeats Mercians to become overlord of England.

849 Birth of Alfred the Great.

867 Danes capture York and ravage Northumbria and Mercia.

870 Danes conquer East Anglia.

871 Saxons under Ethelred and Alfred defeat Danes at Ashdown. Alfred succeeds to throne of Wessex on Ethelred's death.

878 Danes attack Alfred at Chippenham. He is forced to flee to Athelney. Defeats Danes at Ethandune. Danelaw established.

886 Alfred recaptures London from Danes.

899 Death of Alfred.

899–925 Alfred's son Edward and Edward's sister Ethelflaed regain Mercia from the Danes.

925–40 Edward's son Athelstan becomes King of all England.

937 Athelstan's great victory at Brunanburh over the Scots and Irish and Norwegian Vikings.

959–75 Peaceful reign of Edgar.

978 Edgar's son Edward murdered. Ethelred 'the Unready' becomes king.

980 Major Danish assaults on English coast.

1002 Ethelred orders massacre of Danes.

1003 Terrible revenge of Sweyn of Denmark.

1013 Ethelred flees to Normandy.

1014 Death of Sweyn. Restoration of Ethelred.

1016 On death of Ethelred, Edmund Ironside becomes king. Opposed by Canute, Sweyn's son. Death of Edmund. Canute reigns over England and Denmark.

1035 Death of Canute. His son Harold succeeds him.

1040–42 Reign of Harold's half-brother, Harthacnut.

1042–66 Reign of Edward the Confessor

1064 Harold at Duke William of Normandy's Court. The disputed oath of Harold to make William king

1066 Death of Edward. Harold made king. Defeats Norwegian invasion at Stamford Bridge. William defeats Harold at Hastings

New words

Bretwalda Name given to a king who claimed to be overlord of the whole of Saxon England—even if he did not really rule the whole island. Offa of Mercia was a bretwalda in the eighth century.

Churls Freemen who were not noblemen. They owed the king military service in a crisis.

Danelaw The northern, central and eastern parts of Anglo-Saxon England in which Danish laws and customs were observed.

Franks Germanic people who overran Gaul after Rome fell. They gave their name to France.

Fryd All freemen in Saxon England had to serve in the Fryd or local militia when called upon to do so.

Gaul Consisted roughly of France and Belgium, plus parts of Germany, Holland and Switzerland.

Hide A Saxon land measurement. It varied from 24 to 48 hectares (60 to 120 acres) depending on the part of England.

Housecarls The military bodyguard of the kings of England in the eleventh century.

Mercia One of the great Saxon kingdoms, occupying the land between Wales and East Anglia and the Thames and the Humber.

Synod A council of leaders of the churches—as in the Synod of Whitby in 664.

Thanes Saxon landowners, who were also noblemen and warriors.

Thor The Germanic god of thunder, second only in importance to Woden.

Wergild The money a killer was forced to pay for his crime, the amount depending on the victim's rank.

Wessex Became the leading English kingdom in Alfred's time. At its greatest it consisted of the whole of south England from Cornwall to Essex.

Witan or **Witenagemot** The chief advisers to Saxon kings, drawn from the ranks of noblemen and senior clergy.

Woden or **Odin** The greatest of the Saxon's gods before they were converted to Christianity.

Picture Acknowledgements

Mansell Collection 52; all other photographs and black and white line drawings from British Museum/Wayland (Publishers) Ltd.

Further information

Places to visit

Museums Every county in Britain has dozens of museums open to the public, far too many to list here. By far the largest collection of Anglo-Saxon artefacts, including the beautiful treasures found at the Sutton Hoo ship burial site, can be found in the British Museum in London. However, the Saxons were active in most parts of England for over 600 years, so you should be able to find something about them at your nearest museum.

Famous sites The Saxons were not great builders or town dwellers, so little remains of their architecture today. Churches still standing from the Saxon period include the wooden church at Greensted in Essex and the stone church at Bradford-on-Avon in Wiltshire. The remains of the great monastery on Lindisfarne in Northumbria can also still be seen. Winchester was Alfred's capital, so this town has more than its fair share of Saxon remains—as well as a magnificent Victorian statue of Alfred in the market place. Write to the National Trust, enclosing a stamped, addressed envelope for a list of Saxon sites and remains near your home.

Libraries The local library can always give information about the best places to visit, both near your home and farther afield. Most libraries have a section on local history. Try to discover what the Saxons were up to in your area.

Books

Brown, David, *Anglo-Saxon England* (Bodley Head, 1978)

Hamilton, J., and Sorrell, A., *Saxon England* (Lutterworth)

Humble, Richard, *The Saxon Kings* (Weidenfeld and Nicolson, 1980)

Loyn, Henry, *The Norman Conquest* (Hutchinson University Library, 1965)

Page, R. I., *Life in Anglo-Saxon England* (Batsford)

Purves, Amanda, *Growing up in a Saxon Village* (Wayland, 1978)

Triggs, Tony, *The Saxons* (Macdonald & Co., 1979)

Wood, Michael, *In Search of the Dark Ages* (Ariel Books, BBC, 1982)

Woodruff, Douglas, *Alfred the Great* (Weidenfeld and Nicolson, 1974)

Index